The ZOO
in the garden
Discover the animals which live in your garden

David Taylor & Mike Birkhead

Introduction

Y ou may not know it, but you share your garden with lots of other living creatures – you can observe *THE ZOO IN THE GARDEN* from your doorstep.

Many of the animals in the garden seem common or everyday, but in fact they are part of an intricate web of life, each an expert surviving in its own style. So read on and find out about what lives in YOUR garden.

First published in Great Britain in 1987
Reprinted in paperback in 1988
by Boxtree Limited

Text copyright © 1987 by David Taylor
Photographs copyright © 1987 by Mike Birkhead

ISBN 1 85283 020 4

Front cover illustration by David Quinn
Edited by Graham Eyre
Designed by Grahame Dudley
Typeset by Servis Filmsetting Limited, Manchester

Printed in Italy by New Interlitho S.p.A. - Milan

for Boxtree Limited, 36 Tavistock Street,
London WC2E 7PB

Acknowledgement
Photo on page 30 courtesy Oxford Scientific Films

Contents

Abbreviations

mm millimetre
cm centimetre
m metre
km kilometre
ha hectare
gm gram
kg kilogram

The Blue Tit

One of the handsomest of Britain's garden birds is this little dandy in its blue, yellow, black and white gear. If blue tits were a rare tropical species, folk would no doubt praise their beauty more loudly. As it is, the blue tit is the fourth most common bird to be seen in gardens in Britain. Only the blackbird, starling and house sparrow are more common.

The name 'blue tit' is a shortened form of 'blue titmouse' and 'titmouse' comes from Old English. 'Tit' means tiny and 'mouse' (nothing to do with Mickey Mouse!) is a corruption of 'mose', meaning a small bird. Tits, of which there are 42 species worldwide, are typical insect-eating birds of scrub and woodland. Our friend the blue tit occurs widely throughout Europe and Asia.

The blue tit is ever active, tending to flit about from branch to branch, but able to fly long distances too. It is an expert at hanging upside-down, which enables it to hunt caterpillars on the underside of leaves. You can watch its acrobatics for yourself if you have a hanging container of bird food (nuts, suet or one of the special mixtures available from the pet or garden shop) in your garden or back-yard – especially in the winter months, when there are not many insects about and blue tits rely more on seeds and berries for food. At the end of summer, blue tits tend to leave the garden and go hunting in groups in woodland, but they are back as soon as the winter cold sets in.

A pair of blue-tit parents feeding their nestlings gather caterpillars at a rate of around 1 per minute. That means that over the whole period of raising their chicks they catch about 10,000 caterpillars! Another thing blue tits like is cream. They are often seen making short work of milk-bottle tops and helping themselves to the cream at the top of the bottle.

Blue-tit eggs are laid in clutches averaging 10 in number, but they can range from as few as 6 to as many as 24. The eggs, which are white with reddish-brown spots, are laid in April or May and hatch at a time when there are lots of caterpillars around for the chicks to eat. The incubation period – the time it takes for the eggs to hatch – is around 12–14 days and only the female sits on the eggs to hatch them.

About 1 month after the eggs hatch you may be lucky enough to watch the young birds trying to pluck up courage to leave the nest for the first time. To tempt her youngsters to fly, the mother bird sits on a convenient perch outside the nest with a plump caterpillar in her beak. She gives lots of encouragement to her children, saying in effect, 'Come on! You can do it, and here's the prize for the first one to prove it!' The first fledgling to leave the nest is the one who hesitates the most, but as soon as it

A blue tit, the fourth commonest bird in our garden, takes wing

takes the plunge the others usually all fly out at once.

Like other tits, the blue tit nests in a hole in a tree-trunk or, if you are lucky, in your garden nest-box. The nest, which must be dry and draught-proof is snugly lined with shreds of wool, feathers, hair, dried grass and moss. Nest-boxes should have a hole, metal-rimmed to prevent squirrels or

Blue tits welcome feeding in winter

woodpeckers from making it bigger, no more than 2.8 cm across (to keep out starlings and sparrows). Excellent ones can be obtained from the Royal Society for the Protection of Birds. The box should be placed in a position facing away from the prevailing winds at a height of between 1.5 and 2 m with plenty of space around – blue tits like to keep an eye open for their enemies.

Mother as flying-instructor!

Nest-boxes need sound construction

The Hedgehog

The hedgehog is not found in America but is widespread across Europe (except for most of Scandinavia and Iceland), Africa and Asia. There are 12 different species of hedgehog, including the *Western European* (the welcome visitor to our garden), the *long-eared hedgehog* and the *desert hedgehog*. The hedgehog is Britain's heaviest insectivore (insect-eating animal), weighing up to 1.4 kg, and measuring up to 30 cm in length. Hedgehog spines are actually very

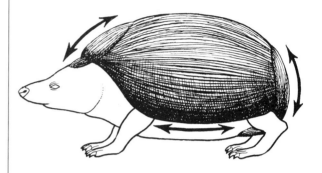

The muscle-shield of the hedgehog

strong and flexible hairs and each adult animal sports about 6000 of them. They are 2–3 cm long, and each has a ball-like root to take shocks and a muscle that can pull it upright when the hedgehog is alarmed. Hedgehogs curl up into a ball at any sign of danger; that's why so many are tragically squashed on our roads. To curl up, a hedgehog uses a big oval shield of muscles that lies beneath the skin, over the back and down the sides of the body from head to tail. By

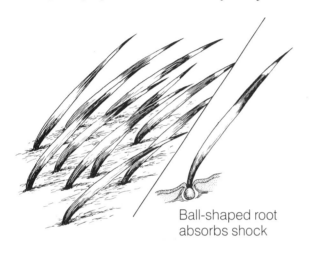

Ball-shaped root absorbs shock

The shock-absorbing spine of a hedgehog

Heading for trouble

drawing in this shield, rather like pulling on the draw-string of a bag, the animal is instantly transformed into a spiky ball.

Hedgehogs are a gardener's friend, feeding on grubs, snails, caterpillars and other pests. Their favourite dish is worms, but they will also eat insects, woodlice, spiders, snails, frogs, toads, lizards and snakes, as well as berries, seeds or fallen fruit, though they do *not*, despite the charming legend, roll about in orchards spearing apples and pears on their prickles and then carrying them off to their larders. If you wish to put out food for a visiting hedgehog, try a saucer of milk, a bit of tinned cat or dog food, hard-boiled egg or cheese scraps. Hedgehogs do take wild birds' eggs if they come across them, but I don't believe they enter hen pens and steal or devour unbroken hens' eggs. As for the belief that hedgehogs suckle milk from cows, I think that's nonsense too. But sometimes a hedgehog may come across a cow with a little milk oozing from the teat of a full udder and

Our friend relishes some cat food

lap up the drops.

Hedgehogs are very resistant to many kinds of poison. They can survive the bites of snakes that would kill 10 men and can eat wasps and bees without apparently being troubled by the insects' stings. They are also very noisy: they snort, hiss, cough cackle, puff, grunt and scream. Nobody who has never heard a hedgehog would believe how noisy it can be. Hedgehogs have fairly good eyesight, but scientists report that they see the world only in shades of yellow! Their senses of hearing and smell are wonderfully well developed. When a hedgehog starts sniffing about, its nose begins to run and this helps the lining of its nostrils to pick up more efficiently the scents in the air.

Hedgehogs are fine swimmers but don't usually take a dip unless they have to. They are also surprisingly good climbers, and when they want to descend they simply let themselves roll

Hedgehogs are quite good climbers

and large birds of prey (such as eagles) may sometimes be successful in forcing the ball open.

Hedgehogs hibernate in the winter, usually going to sleep in October and waking up in April. They pick a snug place called a 'hibernaculum' in a pile of dried leaves or a hole in a bank that they line with moss, bracken and leaves. To save energy and make sure the food stored in its body lasts till spring, the animal allows its temperature to drop and its heartbeat and breathing-rate slow right down. Beneath the skin of the hedgehog's back there is a special hibernation food source in the form of a layer of brown fat. This fat can release heat 20 times faster than ordinary fat and acts as if controlled by a thermostat. The lower the outside temperature, the more heat the brown fat releases into the sleeping hedgehog's body.

In spring a mother hedgehog makes

down, using their spines as shock-absorbers. Few enemies can penetrate the spiky defensive ball of a curled-up hedgehog. Foxes and dogs stand little chance. Badgers, polecats or martens

Napping away the winter months

A prickly defensive ball

her nest in some quiet spot, which may, if you are lucky, be beneath the floor of a garden shed. The baby hedgehogs are born between May and July, with a second litter sometimes produced during August and September after a pregnancy period of 30–40 days. There are normally 3–7 blind and deaf babies in a litter, each of them weighing about 9 gm. The spines of a newborn baby hedgehog are pale, soft and rubbery and are flattened into the skin, which is especially soggy with a high water content. 1½–3 days after birth a second layer of spines begins to grow through the first spines, which are now standing upright. A baby hedgehog cannot roll into a ball until it is about 10 days old.

If you handle a hedgehog – perhaps nursing an injured one – be careful of any fleas and other parasites that there may be on the skin between the spines.

The Mole

The mole is that curious little fellow whose activities make lumps on the lawn. Because it works underground in the dark, and so is rarely seen, the mole is the least known of British garden mammals, though to my mind that makes it one of the most intriguing. It used to be trapped a lot for its velvety fur, used to make coats and trousers, but happily that has nearly stopped.

There are a number of different species of mole. The only one who lives in Britain is the *European mole*. In Spain, the Balkans and Turkey is found the *Mediterranean* mole, and the *Roman mole* lives in Italy and the Balkans. One of the most curious species is the *star-*

pointed muzzle is hairless except for the specialized, highly sensitive whiskers and can be wiggled about.

Moles have tiny but completely formed eyes. They cannot see very well, but their eyes are sensitive to changes in the brightness of light. Moles, which have no external ears, have a poorly developed sense of hearing, as you would expect of a creature who lives mostly underground, but they need and have a very good sense of smell. Glands in the animal's groin produce a smelly substance which is smeared by the belly fur onto the floor of the mole's underground tunnels, as a chemical sign that they are private property. The smell fades quite quickly and must be renewed regularly to keep up the effect. The most powerful sense of the mole, however, is that of touch. Life underground depends on a highly developed ability to feel your way round and recognize obstacles. The mole's

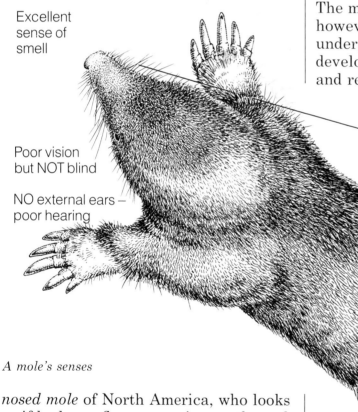

Excellent sense of smell

Poor vision but NOT blind

NO external ears – poor hearing

Highly touch-sensitive whiskers

A mole's senses

nosed mole of North America, who looks as if he has a flower growing on the end of his snout.

A mole's body is long and perfectly shaped for the job of tunnelling. Its colour is a uniform black or dark grey with a short fur whose hairs are of even length and can lie flat in any direction (again, useful for tunnelling). The long,

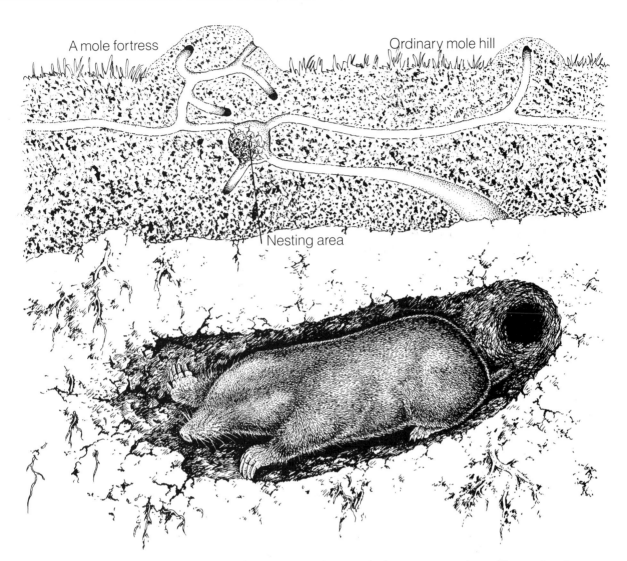

A mole fortress   Ordinary mole hill

Nesting area

muzzle has nerve-endings and there are prominent, very sensitive whiskers on the muzzle and tail.

The powerful digging ability of the mole lies in its sturdy fore-limbs, which are always turned outwards and have five strong, long claws. Moles dig permanent tunnels beneath the soil, with a central nest area lined with grass and leaves. There are occasional shafts up to the surface. Molehills are the earth thrown up on the surface from these shafts. Sometimes in damp soils a special sort of molehill, the fortress, is built to contain the central nesting-area. Tunnels may be up to 1 m deep, and usually the area in which one mole makes its tunnels do not overlap much with the territories of other moles. Moles live alone except in the mating

A mole is an expert miner. He constructs his own underground system

season, though they do seem to be aware of the presence of other moles nearby. Occasionally if there is a drought they are forced to leave their tunnel system and travel perhaps as far as 1 km to find water, a journey which may take them across the territories of up to 10 other moles. When one mole dies or is removed from its patch, its scent fades rapidly and the chemical warning telling other moles to keep away disappears. Other moles quickly take over the property. Sometimes one neighbour takes over the whole territory. Sometimes it is split up among several moles. There may be 5–25 moles per hectare of land, depending upon the soil quality, drainage and the availablity of food. Moles outside the mating season are very unfriendly and fight furiously if they come across other moles.

A mole feeds on worms, slugs, beetles and insect larvae, most of which it finds as it patrols its tunnel system. If not enough food is available, the mole may dig some new tunnels. One adult animal can eat up to 50 gm of worms per day and it will store living worms (paralysed but not killed by having their heads bitten off) in a larder chamber near to the nest. This is done particularly in late autumn as a source of food during the winter.

Moles are active day and night. In

A rare sight! A mole above ground

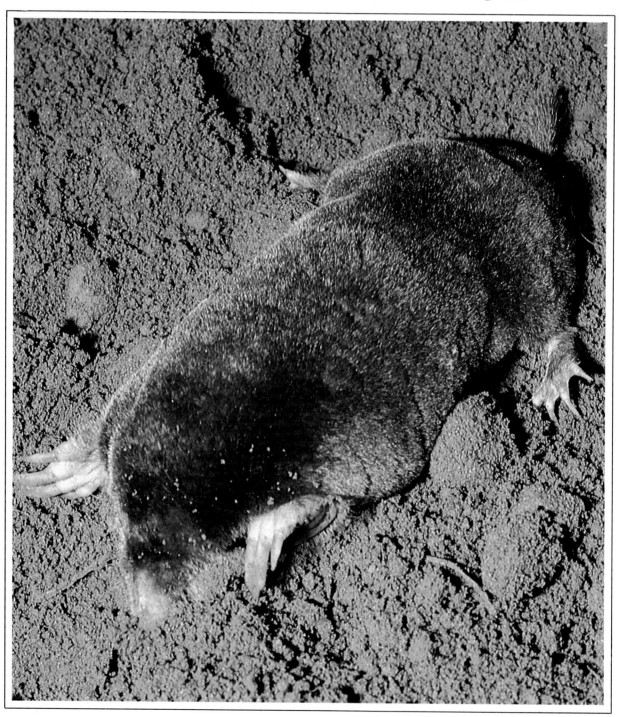

A mole's skin is soft as velvet

winter both males and females work in the tunnels and sleep in their nests in 4-hour spells, which begin when they leave the nest around sunrise. Females do this all year round except in summer, when they are suckling their young and need to go back to the nest more often. During spring, males tend to sleep for short periods in their tunnels and spend much of the rest of their time looking for a mate. At this time they may not visit their nests for days on end. In summer they go back to the pattern of 4 hours' work, 4 hours' sleep, and then in autumn they become lazier and are active for only 2 periods of 4 hours a day. You might wonder how scientists have learnt all this about the mole's underground daily routine. The answer is that they have attached harmless radio transmitters to captured moles; the transmitters tell the scientists what the moles are doing once they have been set free again.

British moles mate between March and June. Surprisingly, since the mole lives underground, the breeding activity is controlled by the amount of daylight!

We assume that the mole detects this when it comes to the surface, as it occasionally does when looking for nesting material, and that daylight acts as a signal to the mole's body that it is time to mate if a partner can be found. The young are born in litters of 2–7 after a pregnancy of 1 month. They are born naked but develop fur by the end of their second week of life. Their eyes open at the end of the third week and they suckle their mother's milk for a total of 4–6 weeks. Then they leave their mother's nest and wander off above ground in search of territory they can dig and claim for their own. It is at this time that large numbers (perhaps over half) of young moles are caught and killed by their enemies, including man. Moles are regarded as pests by gardeners and groundsmen, not only because of the damage molehills do to lawns and sports fields, but also because tunnelling by moles can harm the roots of young plants. Traps and poisons are used in attempts to kill moles.

A mole catcher

The Blackbird

Widespread and numerous in Great Britain, with even more migrating across the English Channel during the winter, this wonderful songbird (I vote it the best of native British songsters) is familiar to everyone. The male is easily recognizable – black with a yellow bill and a yellow ring around the eye. The female is perhaps less easily identified, being dark brown with a pale throat, dark bill and again a yellow ring around the eye. Young birds resemble the females but are generally paler and more mottled. Oddly enough, white blackbirds sometimes occur, though nearly all of these are only partly white, not true albinos (creatures lacking all colour).

Blackbirds are members of the thrush family, which includes 63 different species worldwide. They are intelligent birds that clearly regard the garden as their own and have little fear of human beings. They hop about the lawn and flowerbeds, stopping from time to time to cock their head and listen for the sound of worms moving underground. (They have very sharp hearing.) If they hear anything they will do a bit of digging, making shallow scrapes with their feet and pecking at the ground with their bill. They turn over leaves looking for insects and snails and search bushes and low trees for soft fruit. They tend to fly low, swerving

A male blackbird in typical pose

effortlessly round bushes and landing
with tails held up and wings drooping.
   Blackbirds are very territorial: they
keep to what they consider their own
plot of land, and chase other blackbirds
off. So, if you have a pair of blackbirds
in your garden, you will see a lot of
them. If you have a garden pool or
birdbath you will be able to see your
blackbirds taking their daily bath and
obviously enjoying it. A blackbird
having a bath sits well down in the
water, fluffing out its feathers, lifting
and flapping its wings, flicking water
over its back with its beak and then
nibbling at its breast plumage. It's all
done in quick fussy bursts, after which
the bird flies off to its favourite spot for
drying and preening – a branch or place
on the fence close by. Shaking itself and
fluffing up its feathers, the bird turns its
head and prods with its beak at its
preen gland, near the base of its tail.
This gland contains waterproofing oil,
which the prodding releases. The beak
transfers the oil to the wing and body
feathers, smearing them with a fine

Blackbirds love berries

*The preen gland of a bird. It provides
the oil for waterproofing*

The preen gland here
contains waterproofing oil

'Anting' – to keep down parasites

A female on her deep nest of grass and leaves

coating in a rapid series of nibbling movements.

In warm weather the blackbird will also do a bit of garden sunbathing, and, if there's a patch of sand or dust around, it will take the opportunity to have a dustbath, which keeps the feathers in good condition. You may also see a blackbird crouching with wings spread in a dry part of the garden allowing ants to run all over it. This apparently strange behaviour, called 'anting', is a form of pest control: the ants secrete an acid from glands at the rear of their abdomens and this kills off unwanted guests of the blackbird such as feather mites.

At breeding-time, blackbirds build a deep nest of grass and leaves, usually lightly cemented with mud and situated in a bush, climbing plant or garden shed. Nesting occurs earlier in gardens than in woodlands. The eggs, which are light blue-green with reddish speckles, are laid between March and July in 2 or 3 clutches of 3–6 eggs. The female incubates the eggs and the youngsters start to fly at about 2 weeks old.

The old nursery-rhyme 'Sing a Song of Sixpence' mentions 'four and twenty blackbirds baked in a pie'. Many old nursery rhymes are like secret messages that you cannot understand unless you know the code, and this is true of 'Sing a Song of Sixpence'. It may refer to King Henry VIII, who in the sixteenth century decided to close down all the monasteries in England. The blackbirds may be the monasteries' choirs; the Queen in the parlour eating bread and honey may be Catherine of Aragon, Henry's first wife; and the maid hanging out the clothes may be Henry's second wife, Ann Boleyn.

A children's rhyme with a hidden meaning

The Ladybird

Not many people like insects, but, then, most people think of insects as nasty creepy-crawlies. In fact there are some very beautiful insects, such as butterflies, dragonflies and scarab beetles (which come from the East and have shells so lovely that they have been used as jewellery). These are the sort of insects nearly everyone likes, though few realize that they are insects. The same is true of the beetle called the ladybird. The 'lady' in its name refers to the Virgin Mary ('Our Lady') and the

It is thought that this verse refers to the old practice of setting fire to hop fields in September after the harvest.

In Northumberland in the north of England, where an old name for the ladybird is the 'reed sodger', there is a similar tradition. You throw the ladybird into the air and say,

Reed, reed sodger fly away
And make the morn a sunny day.

French children recite a verse that

A seven-spot out and about

'bird' here just means a flying creature.

If a ladybird lands on you, then according to an old English tradition you are supposed not to flick it off but to blow gently and say,

Ladybird, ladybird, fly away home.
Your house is on fire and your
children are gone.

warns the ladybird of a Turkish invasion and the slaughter of all her young ones. Everywhere the ladybird is regarded as a good and useful creature, feeding as it does on both the larvae and adult forms of aphids – pests such as the greenfly. The number of spots on a ladybird's wings was thought to indicate

Antenna

Head

Thorax

Abdomen under wings

6 legs

The basic insect body and a ladybird compared. The ladybird uses one pair of wings as a wing-case

the future price of wheat: each spot represented an extra shilling for a bushel of corn (5 pence for 36 litres). It was considered particularly unlucky to kill a ladybird, and in East Anglia, for example, if one were accidentally killed it would be carefully buried and the grave stamped upon 3 times while the rhyme 'Ladybird, ladybird, fly away home' was recited. At one time the yellow liquid which the insect secretes when alarmed was considered an effective treatment for toothache. The sufferer rubbed his finger on the ladybird's legs and then rubbed the liquid onto the aching tooth.

Like other insects, ladybirds are creatures that live on land, have no backbones or lungs, and breathe through a system of simple air-tubes that open onto the body surface. The body is divided into three main parts – the head, the chest or thorax, and the abdomen. It is covered by a horny coating or external skeleton which is

shed now and again to allow the insect to grow. The head carries a pair of feelers or antennae and there are three pairs of feeding appendages. Generally there are one or two pairs of wings arising from the thorax and three pairs of legs.

True beetles, of which there are around 300,000 species, form the biggest group of insects, and range in size from 0.5 mm to over 15 cm long. The largest are the *Goliath beetles*, which are some of the biggest insects alive. The Latin name (*Coleoptera*) of the beetle family means 'sheath wings' and refers to the fore-wings, which form an armoured covering for the delicate hind wings used for flying. Beetles live mainly on the ground and have a heavily armed head with a mouth formed for biting and compound eyes, which allow the beetle

The ladybird is a carnivore, not a plant-eater

to see almost all the way round itself.

There are 400 species of ladybird in the world and there are 41 species in Great Britain. All are round in outline with hemispherical bodies (like an up-turned pudding bowl) where the head is concealed beneath the thorax. Most are brightly coloured and spotted. They have short and nimble legs. Nearly all are carnivorous, which means that they eat other animals. Ladybirds are indeed gardeners' friends, though there are a few exceptions: for instance, the squash ladybird of the United States damages pumpkins. The striking colours and designs of ladybirds serve to warn creatures that might be tempted to eat them that they contain poisonous chemicals, though no human can be harmed by handling them.

If you look carefully you may be able to identify 5 or 6 different species of ladybird busily going about their business of keeping down the greenfly in your garden. One of the commonest is the *seven-spot ladybird*, which is about 6 mm long and has 3 black spots on each of its bright red wing-cases, with the

seventh spot shared between them. You will often find this ladybird resting under a flower-head. A plant it is particularly fond of is hogweed. The biggest ladybird in Britain is the *eyed ladybird*, about 8 mm long. It is frequently found on pine-trees and displays 7 or 8 spots on each wing-case. The most common British ladybird is the *two-spot*. Generally it has one spot on each wing-case, but just to confuse you it may have a total of 4 or even 6! Some varieties reverse the colouring by having red spots on black wing-cases. The *ten-spot ladybird* is also quite common and tends to favour woodland. It possesses red, brown or black wing-cases with yellow, black or orange spots. It is about 4 mm long and has tiny yellow legs. In southern parts of England the *fourteen-spot ladybird* can sometimes be found. It is about 4 mm long and has very bright and distinct yellow and black markings. Smaller still at 3 mm long is the *twenty-two spot ladybird*, which has 11 black spots on each yellow or pale orange wing-case. It can be found in certain areas of England, Wales and eastern Ireland.

A twenty-two spot ladybird

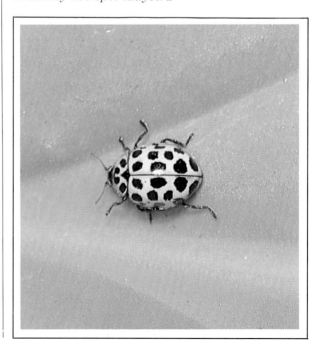

A fourteen-spot ladybird with spots fused together

The *twenty-four spot ladybird* is an interesting creature, being a vegetarian that feeds on clover and similar plants. Despite its name, it has a total of 16–20 irregularly sized spots on its orange wing-cases. It is another of the smaller ladybirds, at around 3 mm long.

Although ladybirds tend to remain calm with their wing-cases closed when you pick one up or gently touch one sitting on a flower, they are very good at flying. Their finely veined transparent hind wings can carry them over vast distances. Some ladybirds migrate to Britain from continental Europe and occasionally a swarm of them can number tens of thousands. If they are unlucky enough to meet with bad weather on the way, so many of them may fall into the sea that the water seems to turn red.

Adult ladybirds hibernate over winter in Great Britain. Look for them beneath pieces of loose bark or on the underside of dry and sheltered window-sills. Many die of diseases such as fungus infections. They also have an enemy in the form of a wasp-like insect that lays its eggs within the body of the adult ladybird. When the eggs hatch into grubs they feed on the flesh of the ladybird but do not necessarily kill it. Sometimes you will see the tiny pupa of the parasite still attached to a ladybird as it works its way along a stem full of greenfly.

Each female ladybird lays about 200 eggs, generally on the underside of leaves and conveniently near to greenfly colonies. Larvae emerge from the eggs and begin feeding on the aphids, killing perhaps 30 or 40 every day. The larval ladybird, a slate-blue caterpillar-like creature with yellow spots, grows to be much longer than the adult beetle at around 12–13 mm. In the 3 weeks before the larva turns into a pupa it eats it way through many hundreds of aphids. At the end of the 3 weeks the larva shrinks and rounds off into a hard-cased grey and yellow oval pupa, rather like a button. The pupa is firmly attached to a stem of leaf, generally in an exposed position, and stays there until the adult ladybird emerges from it.

The baby is longer than the adult!

The Centipede and Millipede

Do a bit of digging and you will soon enough come across a flattish, rusty-brown, many-legged creature that wriggles artfully away from your trowel or spade. It is the centipede, and, like the ladybird, it is a friend of the gardener. Centipedes are not insects – though, funnily enough, they are more closely related to insects than to the somewhat similar millipedes. There are around 3000 species of centipede. Almost all of them live on the land and have elongated bodies made up of many segments, with a distinct head, one pair of feelers or antennae, and a single pair of legs on each segment. As most species are carnivorous, preying upon small animals such as slugs and insects, they help to control plant pests in the garden. Like insects, spiders and Crustaceans (such as lobsters and crabs)

centipedes have their skeletons on the outside of the body in the form of a tough outer shell or 'exoskeleton'. This cannot stretch, so the centipede has to shed its body covering from time to time to be able to grow. The cast-off outer skeletons are whitish and hollow, and look rather 'ghostly'. You may be able to find them lying in the garden.

Although the word 'centipede' means 'a hundred feet', the number of feet varies from 34 and 254, depending on the species. The longest known species is a 46-legged giant living in the jungles of South America, which when fully grown is about 40 cm long but can reach 90 cm! Big centipedes such as this are fully grown at around 4 years old and may live for 10 years. British centipedes, of which there are 44 species, don't get

The centipede is blind as a bat

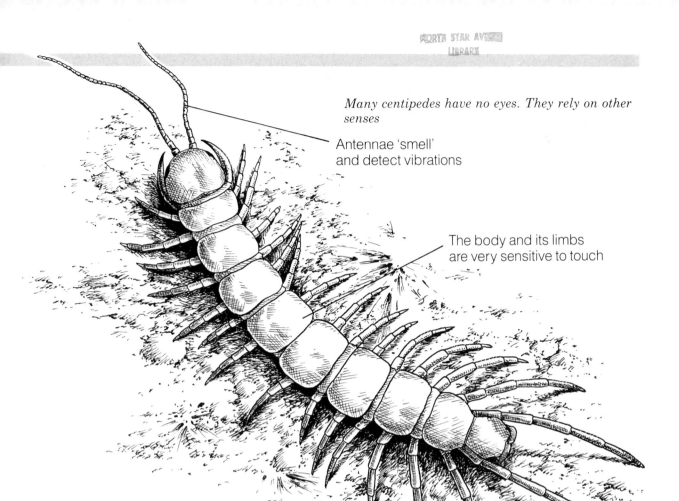

Many centipedes have no eyes. They rely on other senses

Antennae 'smell'
and detect vibrations

The body and its limbs
are very sensitive to touch

much bigger than about 10 cm, while the smallest is a mere 5–10 mm long. Centipedes seem to move quite fast, but probably no species can leg it at more than 5 miles (8 km) per hour. The first pair of legs on a centipede are not used for walking but have been modified into poison fangs. These are used to paralyse and kill prey. Though most centipedes are harmless to human beings, there are a few foreign species now resident in Britain which can give a most unpleasant nip.

Centipedes are nocturnal. Sunlight and heat are lethal to them. Unlike insects, they do not have within their outer skin a waxy waterproof layer that retains body moisture. A few hours of exposure to dry or sunny conditions will kill a centipede. This is why you will often find dead centipedes in greenhouses or under sheets of glass. The world of the centipede is one of complete darkness. None of the British species has any form of eye. To catch their prey, centipedes rely on their

highly developed sense of touch, their ability to pick up vibrations and the chemical detecting-cells in their antennae. Although most centipedes feed only on other creatures, such as woodlice, slugs, insects and smaller centipedes, there is one species at least that can damage growing celery and lettuce.

Female centipedes lay eggs one at a time. The egg is then handled by special claws at the back of the body and is smeared with a special sticky liquid to which bits of soil cling, making it hard to see. The egg is then hidden in the earth or under leaf mould and another egg is laid. From the eggs tiny but perfectly formed baby centipedes with fewer legs than the adult eventually emerge.

Keep your eyes open and you may be

able to recognize several different kinds of centipede in your garden. The *common centipede* is around 3 cm long, possesses 60 legs and holds its body rigid when running. (Most other species move with a snaky side-to-side movement.) During the day this centipede is often found beneath stones or bits of wood. Another common species, *Halophilus*, is up to 7 cm long, thin and yellowish, with 160 or more legs. *Necrophloephagus* is a yellowish centipede with a dark brown head. It is about 3.5 cm long and often burrows in gardens.

The centipede should not be confused with another multi-legged creature of the garden, the millipede. The name 'millipede' means 'a thousand feet', but no millipede has anything like that

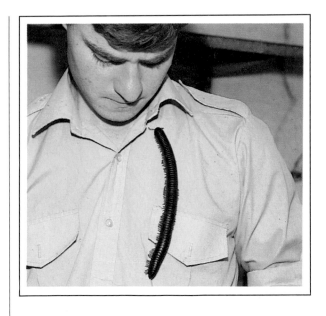

Giant millipedes make harmless pets

Millipedes don't have a thousand legs!

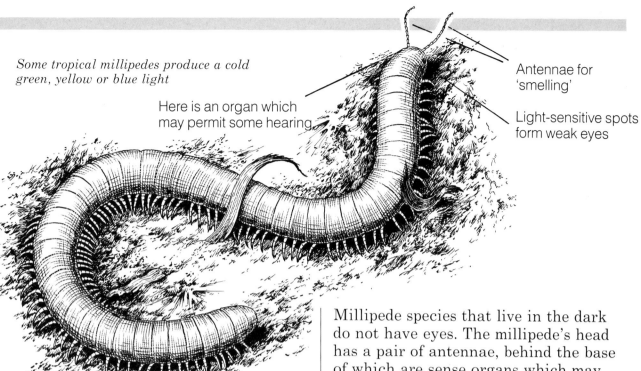

Some tropical millipedes produce a cold green, yellow or blue light

Here is an organ which may permit some hearing

Antennae for 'smelling'

Light-sensitive spots form weak eyes

number of feet! Unlike centipedes, millipedes are almost wholly vegetarian, and, whereas centipedes have one pair of legs on each segment, millipedes boast two pairs. Like centipedes, millipedes live in the soil and under leaf mould. The tiniest are only 2 mm long, but the biggest (which come from the tropics and make excellent cheap exotic pets) can reach 20 cm.

50 species of millipede live in the United Kingdom. One of the commonest is the *black snake millipede*, which grows up to 30 mm long and has 96 pairs of legs. When it is attacked it curls itself up into a flat coil so that its strong exoskeleton can protect its softer under-belly. As it rolls up it secretes a smelly poisonous liquid from a line of glands along the side of its body. This puts off most attackers. Another common British millipede is the *pill millipede* (about 50 mm long), which has a shiny body with broad back and narrow yellow bands. When threatened, it curls itself up into a little ball.

Most species of millipede have eyes, but these, unlike the powerful eyes of insects, are simply light-sensitive spots.

Millipede species that live in the dark do not have eyes. The millipede's head has a pair of antennae, behind the base of which are sense organs which may give the creature some hearing ability. Use a magnifying glass to look at the legs and movement of a millipede. The legs possess 6 or 7 joints and in most species arise close together along the middle of the under-surface. Millipedes do not move quickly but they are certainly graceful, crawling along with lovely wavy movements.

Female millipedes lay eggs from which larvae looking like miniature versions of the adults but with a smaller number of body segments and legs emerge. As the larva grows, new segments develop.

Amazingly, many foreign kinds of millipede can produce light! On the undersurface of their bodies are two kinds of glands. When mixed, the liquid secreted by these glands undergoes a remarkable chemical change, producing bluish, yellowish or greenish light. This light, which was recorded by Christopher Columbus and his companions when they visited Santo Domingo on their first voyage to the New World, has nothing to do with producing heat. It is similar to the light emitted by other kinds of living creature, such as fire-flies. It is a pity that no British variety of millipede shares this ability.

The Butterfly

Butterflies are short-lived but beautiful inhabitants of the summer garden. Despite their name, they have nothing to do with butter! The way in which the butterfly emerges from the husk that was its chrysalis or pupa is rather like something that was dead coming to life, and this is why it reminded people of the idea that when someone dies the 'soul' leaves the body and lives on. Butterflies were even thought of as the carriers of souls.

Moths are similar to butterflies and belong to the same group of insects, *Lepidoptera*; but there are some important differences between them. First, butterflies are active by day, while most moths are more active at night. Secondly, resting moths usually hold their wings spread out, while resting butterflies hold them pressed together. Thirdly, the feelers or antennae of butterflies are slender with blobs on the tips, while those of moths are short and feathery.

Butterflies are true insects and their bodies possess all the basic features of insects, with a body divided into 3 parts: head, thorax (chest) and abdomen, which has 11 rather indistinct segments. 6 legs arise from the thorax and each segment of the abdomen possesses a pair of air-tubes or spiracles opening onto the skin surface, through which the creature breathes. And, of course, they have wings. But there are many special features about butterflies which make them not only the most beautiful but also some of the cleverest creatures in your garden.

In the first place, butterflies have the keenest sense of smell in the animal kingdom. Each antenna has 40,000 tiny receptors linked to nerves for handling general smells. A male butterfly can pick up the scent of a female from as far away as 11 km, yet the total stock of perfume carried by a female is no more than 0.0001 mg! It appears that, when he has picked up the scent of a female, the male starts flying into the wind, which has carried the smell. To help him find his way, he has instruments that

The life-cycle of a butterfly

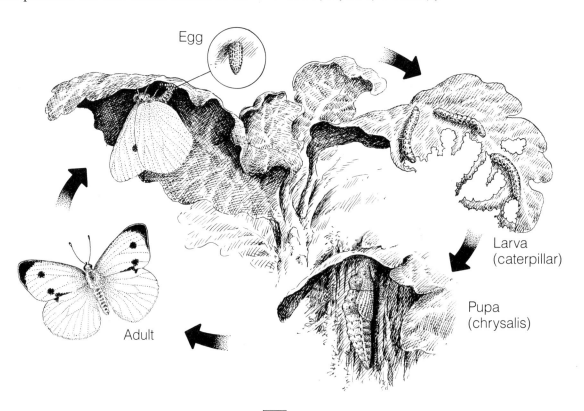

Egg

Larva (caterpillar)

Pupa (chrysalis)

Adult

measure the wind located in joints of his antennae. So that he doesn't miss the female's scent among all the other smells in the air, the male has special receptor cells that react only to the perfume of the female.

Butterflies have 2 compound eyes, like a lot of eyes joined together. They scales. These scales are pegged to the wing like tiles on a roof. Some butterfly wings, particularly in the tropics, shimmer with blue light. This is caused by grooves on the scales, which absorb all colours in the light except blue. Butterflies are very good at flying: some species migrate, and they can travel as

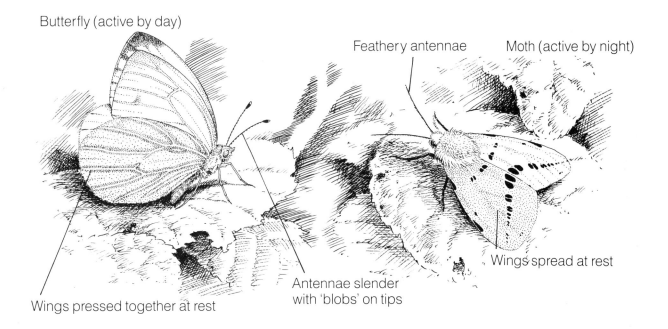

Butterfly (active by day)

Feathery antennae

Moth (active by night)

Wings spread at rest

Antennae slender with 'blobs' on tips

Wings pressed together at rest

are particularly good at receiving red colours, which is important for the pollination of plants such as the Sweet William. Unlike the human eye, the eye of the butterfly is sensitive to ultraviolet light, which allows it to see colours we can't. If a plant reflects ultraviolet light, its colour for a butterfly will be quite different from its colour for us. For instance, the red poppy reflects ultraviolet light, so to a butterfly it is not red at all but a pure ultraviolet, a sort of deep blue.

The glory of both butterflies and moths is, of course, their wings. Their family name, *Lepidoptera*, means 'scale-wings'. If you handle a butterfly gently, you will find your fingers quickly covered with a fine powder that dusts off the wings. Look at the powder under a microscope and you will see that it is made up of beautifully formed little

Differences between moth and butterfly

Sense of direction and smell are superb

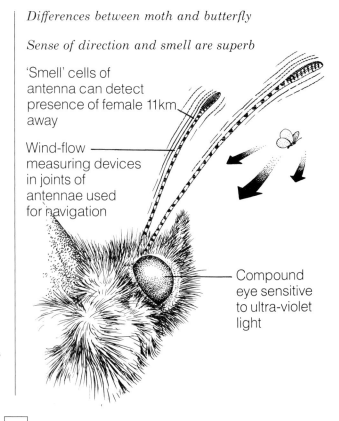

'Smell' cells of antenna can detect presence of female 11km away

Wind-flow measuring devices in joints of antennae used for navigation

Compound eye sensitive to ultra-violet light

far as 3000 km.

Look at the head of a butterfly. At the front of the head is a 'tongue' that when not in use is coiled like a watch-spring. Actually this is a tube that when stretched right out is used to suck nectar from flowers. Almost all butterflies (and moths) feed upon nectar.

Silver studded blues

Occasionally the juices of over-ripe fruit are also taken, particularly by species such as the *red admiral*. One of Britain's rarest and most spectacular butterflies, the *purple emperor*, likes to suck the juices of the rotting bodies of animals.

If you wish to attract butterflies to your garden, you must avoid using sprays that kill insects and weeds. A bank of mixed flowers in a border is very appealing to butterflies, especially if behind it there is a brick wall that heats up in the sun. Different flowers appeal to different butterflies, so, the more varieties you have, the more different types of butterfly you are likely to see. If you can, it is a very good idea to have a patch of wild flowers.

The eggs of butterflies come in various shapes and the designs on their shells can be unbelievably beautiful, but you must look at them under a microscope to see them properly. Some females may lay a thousand or more eggs. The eggs are laid on a plant that the caterpillars can eat after they hatch. Their first meal on hatching, though, is the shell of the egg, which contains vitamins essential to the health of the caterpillars. Only one in every hundred butterfly eggs get to the point of hatching. The rest perish from disease or are eaten by birds, bugs, mites or certain flies. It usually takes 1–2 weeks for the eggs to hatch.

Caterpillars have 3 pairs of true legs attached to the thorax or chest and 5 pairs of temporary legs attached to the abdomen. The legs have hooks or claws for grasping leaves and twigs. The head has powerful cutting jaws, a pair of very short feelers or antennae, and 6 simple light-spot eyes on each side. Along the sides of the body are 9 pairs of small dots: these are breathing holes or spiracles. Beneath the mouth is an opening that leads from the glands that

The beautiful eggs of the small white

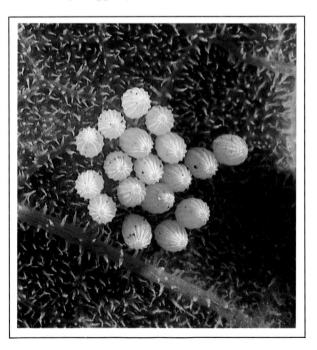

make silk, which is used to make and fix the cocoons in which the pupa or chrysalis changes into a butterfly.

Caterpillars protect themselves from enemies in a whole variety of ways. Some are hairy, some are armed with spikes and spines, and in some tropical varieties the spines are attached to poison glands and can sting. Some caterpillars protect themselves by feeding only at night; others form cases or webs on the leaves. Some hide themselves by having the same pattern or colour as the plant they feed upon. Even so, 99 per cent of caterpillars are eaten by birds and other creatures or die from disease.

As caterpillars grow, they moult their tough skins 4 times. The new skin is soft and stretches, but it soon hardens into a exoskeleton. After the fourth moult the caterpillar changes into a pupa or chrysalis. Some pupae are enclosed in a covering or cocoon of silk, while others are simply glued to a plant or hang from a silken pad. The pupa is a hard casing

Peacock caterpillars on nettles in June

formed from the skin or a caterpillar with the legs glued down into it. Many sorts of chrysalis look like dead leaves or bits of dried stem, to protect them. Within the chrysalis the caterpillar gradually turns into an adult butterfly, and when it is ready the insect breaks out of the chrysalis, pumps liquid into the veins of its wings to stretch them out, and sits for up to 2 hours waiting for them to dry. Then for the first time, it soars into the air, the brand-new wings beating at up to 10 times per second.

The biggest living butterfly is the female *Queen Alexandra birdwing* of New Guinea, which has a wingspan of almost 30 cm! The biggest native British butterfly is the *swallowtail* (7–10 cm), and the smallest is the *small blue* (2–2.5 cm). If you are a real butterfly fan, the best place to go is Brazil, where there are hundreds of species, but there is still plenty of variety in Britain, with 70

The cabbage white

recorded species. Here are some of them, divided into groups by colour.

The *whites* include such species as the *small white, wood white, green-veined white* and the *orange tip*. The most familiar and notorious is the *large cabbage white*, whose caterpillars eat cabbages and other plants. There are 2 generations of large cabbage white in Britain each year, the first between April and June and the second between July and September.
There are several species of *yellow* butterfly, but the one you are most likely to see is the *brimstone*. This is a truly butter-coloured butterfly, and some people believe that it is how the

The brimstone butterfly

butterfly got its name.
All the *brown* butterflies have false 'eye' designs on the upper or lower surfaces of their wings to deter their enemies. The commonest British butterfly is the *meadow brown*. It lives for 1 month and

The meadow brown. Note the 'eyes'

flies on dull and even rainy days. Some of the *blue* butterflies are very rare, but the one you are most likely to see in the garden is the *common blue*.

A large skipper

There are 8 species of British *skipper*. These are small, yellow-brownish butterflies, frequently with white markings. They are fast and quite aggressive, and will chase off other flying insects, including bees.

A summer visitor: the painted lady

The gorgeous comma

The *comma* loves buddleias, asters and Michaelmas daisies. With its wings folded, the adult looks like a dead and ragged leaf.

A red admiral on buddleia flowers

The *red admiral* flies by night as well as day. It often rests and sunbathes, spreading and displaying its gorgeous wings. It delights in feeding on ice-plants, buddleias and Michaelmas daisies in the autumn.

The *painted lady* migrates to Britain from Southern Europe and North Africa in May and June. It is very fond of garden flowers and thistles, but cannot survive the British winter.

The *fritillaries* are orange or brown butterflies with black spots. They prefer woodlands to gardens.

The *peacock* likes stinging nettles, and you should look for its black, hairy caterpillars on these plants in June. The adult enjoys feeding on the sap of ripe fruit in orchards. It gets its name from the eyes on its wings, which are intended to 'stare' at and frighten away enemies.

The glamorous peacock butterfly

The Bee

The bee is the royal emblem of France. Yes, it is true that the emblem is called the fleur-de-lis, which is French for the iris, but this shape was originally meant to represent a flying bee. The old royal robe and banners of France were thickly sewn

The fleur-de-lis: not a plant, but a bee

with golden bees, and when the tomb of the early French king Childeric (436–81 AD) was opened in the seventeenth century it was found to contain 300 bees made of gold.

People like bees because they make honey and pollinate flowers. Everybody knows that they are very busy creatures, and you will often see them working in your garden. Some species,

such as the *honey bee*, live in well-organized colonies or hives. These bees are called 'social' bees, and the females are of 2 types: there are a few 'queen' bees, who can lay eggs, and lots and lots of 'worker' bees, who cannot breed at all. The males are called 'drones'. You may be surprised to learn that most species of bee are 'solitary' bees: they live on their own, and the female makes a nest for her 'brood', the larvae that hatch from the eggs she lays.

Bees are insects and have hairy, plump bodies which are large compared with their wings. The joints of the hind legs are specially big and covered with thick hair, which collects pollen. The eggs of bees are laid singly in chambers or cells, and each bee's nest contains a number of cells; the hive bee's has many thousands. Along with each egg enough food is deposited to feed the larva until it turns into a pupa. Adult bees feed on nectar and pollen from flowers. The larvae also eat pollen and honey, which is made from nectar in the bee's 'honey

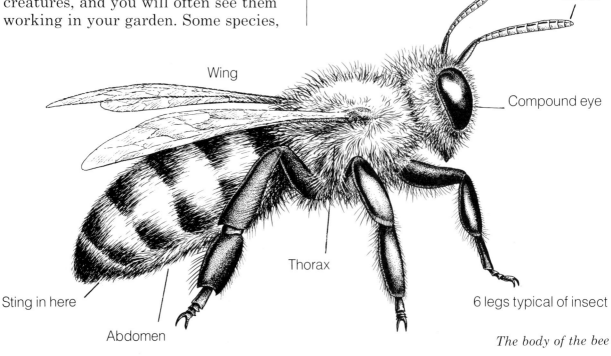

Antenna

Compound eye

Wing

Thorax

6 legs typical of insect

Sting in here

Abdomen

The body of the bee

stomach' and then brought up again at the nest or hive. Honey is a form of concentrated nectar rich in sugars. Pollen contains lots of protein.

Solitary bees make their nests in a variety of places. Some make burrows in the ground, with single cells leading off a main passage. Others make use of spaces they find in buildings, walls, trees or bushes. They may even use keyholes or empty snail shells!

Honey bees build the cells of the hive out of scales of wax, which they produce from glands on the under-surface of their abdomens. They shape the wax by lifting it on their legs and kneading it with their jaws. To seal cracks in the honeycomb, bees like to collect resin from trees. If there are no trees available, they may fetch warm tar from a nearby road. To soften the wax of the honeycomb, water is needed, and every day some bees will go in search of ponds and puddles. The cells are built very carefully. The bee measures everything it does using its antennae and the sensitive bristles on its abdomen. If the honeycomb is damaged, the bees at once start making repairs.

The bee that you see in the garden is a living machine far more complex than

A typical beehive

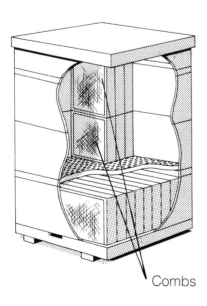

Combs

any rocket or computer. Bees have a perfect sense of temperature and can detect rises or falls of less than 1°C. Temperature control is very important to honey bees, and they have worked out ways of keeping a constant temperature of 35°C in the hive's

A bee-keeper inspects a honeycomb

breeding-cells. In cool weather, worker bees crowd together in their thousands on top of the cells to warm them up. If it goes colder, they huddle closer and cover the brood cells with their bodies to make a living eiderdown. On the other hand, if it is too hot they bring in water and cover the combs with a fine film which they then cause to evaporate by fanning it with their wings. They sit like little ventilators over the cells driving the warm air towards each other and pushing it out again through the entrance.

The compound eye of the bee is made up of 15,000 parts or facets, which are like lots of separate eyes and divide everything the bee sees into a screen of squares. It uses this screen in order to find its way and work out its speed. As the bee flies along, it charts its course in relation to the sun and the way in which what it sees changes on its screen and so tells how fast it is flying.

The bee also has a mechanism that works out air-speed. This is centred in nerves within the joints of the antennae. When the wind bends the antennae, signals are sent into the central computer. By comparing the signals from the antennae with the information from the eye about the bee's flying-speed, the computer works out at once the angle at which the bee should fly. What is more, the eyeball of a bee has rows of tiny hairs where the facets join. These hairs sense air-movements,

carbon dioxide in the air. If the amount rises, it immediately triggers off a rapid fanning motion of the wings. This mechanism is employed by worker bees to ensure that the air in the hive is always fresh. The chemical receptors of the antennae can also pick up the scents of blossoms, and, depending on which antenna picks up the stronger scent, the bee knows which way to fly to find the flowers producing the scent. (If

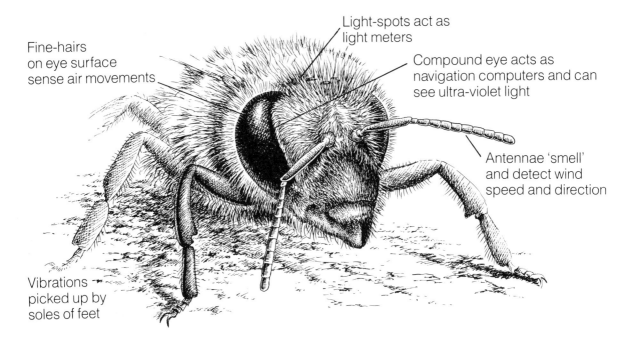

Fine-hairs on eye surface sense air movements

Light-spots act as light meters

Compound eye acts as navigation computers and can see ultra-violet light

Antennae 'smell' and detect wind speed and direction

Vibrations picked up by soles of feet

and in next to no time the bee can correct its flight when it is affected by gusts of wind, so that it is not blown off-course.

In the hairy fur between the bee's compound eyes are 3 tiny eye spots, which are used to measure how light it is (like the lightmeter on a camera). These light meters are very important, because they tell a bee when it is safe to go out in the morning and also when it should return home. The bee's computer tells it how far it is from the hive or nest, and as the light fades the bee can tell when it must leave for home and how fast it must fly to reach there at the right time.

The bee's two antennae have nerve receptors which react to the level of

A bee's senses are truly amazing

both antennae give the same message, the bee is heading in the right direction.) The antennae are not the only way in which bees seek out food flowers. They use their eyes too, and because they (like butterflies) can see ultra-violet light, they see things in a completely different way from us. One colour they cannot see is red, which looks black to them. But, because some flowers that look red to us reflect ultra-violet light, the bee sees them as a deep blue!

Bees cannot hear in the same way as we can, but they can pick up vibrations through the soles of their feet and use vibrations to 'speak' to other bees.

Bees swarming on a tree trunk

Another way in which bees can communicate with each other is through dancing! The other bees watch the dance and get the message at once.

You may one day see bees swarm in your garden. This happens when there are too many bees in a colony. The colony prepares to divide by swarming. Dense balls containing thousands of bees form a swarm and they tend to occur between May and July. You might see them attached to the branch of a tree as a sort of buzzing ball, and sometimes they will build a temporary

A honey bee at work

honeycomb there before setting up the new colony. If bees do swarm in your garden, don't be frightened but leave the bees alone. You should ask a local beekeeper for advice. He may move the swarm, which has to be done very carefully.

Despite all their skills and industry, most bees do not live very long. Honey bees live for only about 1 month in summer. Lots of people think that all the bees they see in the garden are honey bees, but in fact there are over 200 different species of bee in Britain and the honey bee is only one of them. *Bumble bees*, of which there are 18

The same flower visited by a bumble bee

species in Britain, are easily recognized because of their big furry bodies. Like honey bees, they are social bees. Each colony has one queen, plus lots of female workers and male drones.

Everyone knows that bees can sting. The sting is a sort of poison needle that sticks out from the end of the abdomen. Worker bees use it as a means of defence and always die after stinging, as the sting is barbed (like an arrow) and cannot be pulled out when it has been used. Queen bees that have not bred and laid eggs have unbarbed stings, used for killing other queens.

The Frog

To me frogs and toads are fascinating animals. They are quiet, neat, slightly comical creatures and they live in ponds. You often see frogs in your garden, even if there is no pond or pool but just some damp and shady areas.

Frogs are amphibians – creatures that live both on land and in water – but unlike reptiles (such as snakes) they have naked, moist skin which is used in breathing to obtain oxygen. Most young amphibians hatch from eggs that are deposited in water and develop into larvae that breath through external gills in a similar way to fish. They gradually change into animals that can live on land. Their gills disappear and they begin to breathe through their skin and a brand-new pair of lungs.

There are 1800 species of frog and

The common toad

A frog at home

toad in the world today. The biggest frog in the world is the rare *Goliath frog* from Guinea in West Africa. The biggest frog in Britain is the *marsh frog*, which arrived from Hungary in 1935. From the tip of its nose to the base of its rump it measures 10–13 cm, while the biggest native frog, the *common frog*, doesn't

quite reach 10 cm.

Although some toads are long-lived and can perhaps reach 40 years of age, frogs tend not to live anywhere near as long. There may be exceptions (we don't know much about the Goliath frog, for instance), but the limit for the species we know a lot about seems to be about 16 years.

If you pick up a frog, hold it very gently and look at it carefully. Don't keep it in your warm hands for more than a minute or two – such a cool and damp-skinned animal finds it most uncomfortable! The frog has a special kind of tongue which is fixed to the front of the mouth and can be flicked forward. Within the tongue are lots of glands which ooze and make it sticky. When a frog sees an insect, it flicks out its tongue, which sticks to the insect and pulls it back into the frog's mouth. Although adult frogs are carnivores, their larvae (tadpoles) are vegetarians when first hatched and feed on algae, which are tiny plants that grow in water.

Watch a frog sitting quietly, gulping from time to time as its throat pumps up and down. What it is doing is breathing

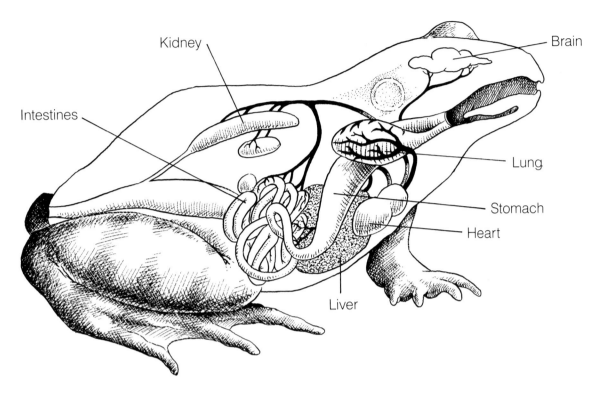

Kidney

Brain

Intestines

Lung

Stomach

Heart

Liver

by swallowing air and squeezing it down into its lungs. As frogs have almost no ribs and no diaphragm (the muscle between chest and abdomen), they can't breathe with their chests.

Frogs have a larynx or voice-box at the top of their windpipe. This is what they use to croak. Some frogs, such as the *edible frog* of continental Europe, have pouches on the sides of their throat which they can blow out to make their croaking louder. Breathing through the skin is even more important for frogs than breathing through their lungs, which they cannot use when hibernating under water.

The eyes of a frog are well developed and have tear-glands and eyelids that close. It has been discovered that usually their eyes do not pick out anything that is not moving. They are programmed, however, to react to blue and green. When they are threatened, blue means water and safety, while green means grass and spells danger. This means that when they are frightened they will even jump at a piece of blue paper, thinking that it is

The basic body plan of a frog

water. Frogs' eyes bulge and make room when a large object is swallowed, as there is no bone between the roof of the mouth and the eye-socket, just thin sheets of soft tissue.

Frogs hear well and their ears are very sensitive to ground vibrations, which are transmitted through the

Frogs can't 'see' anything that doesn't move

forelegs and shoulders. Amphibians are very sensitive to smells in the air and like snakes have the so-called 'Jacobsen's organ', which enables them to tell what is the air by flicking out their tongue.

Frogs are very good at jumping. The record is held by the South African *sharp-nosed frog*, which has been known to cover almost 10 m in three leaps. It is said that this frog can jump 4.57 m in a single leap.

In spring, frogs go back to the pond or pool where they were born. The amount of daylight, and the temperature of the moisture in the air tell them when to move, and they may travel up to 3 km to reach their home pond. Frogs are very clever at finding their way: they recognize landmarks, and some species can tell where to go from the position of

Some frogs can jump over 4½ m

the sun and stars. In autumn they move from their summer haunts to their hibernation sites, which are often the same pond.

During mating, all the senses of the frog come into play. They are attracted by sounds (mating-calls), smells and sight, as well as touch. Male frogs have highly sensitive 'pimples' on their breasts and toes, and females have similar tiny points on their backs. These are stimulated when they are touched. The skin-colour of a frog can change gradually according to where it lives. This change is controlled by a gland in the brain (the pituitary gland), the same one as tells the frog when it is time to go home to mate.

Each species of frog has its own particular voice, and frogs croak and call for a variety of reasons. Male do so to show off during the mating-season and attract females, or to declare

ownership of territory. Distressed and alarmed frogs often cry out, and the delightful, vividly coloured *tree frogs* of the tropics croak for joy when rain falls!

The frog you are most likely to find in your garden is the *common* or *grass frog*, particularly on damp days or at night. This animal has a yellow to greenish-

Frogs mating on Hampstead Heath

brown skin with numerous blotches and stripes and dark markings. Look at the eyes and see how they are set high on the head – perfect for peeping cautiously out of the water. Notice that the pupils in the eyes run from side to side. The common frog tends to live alone outside the mating-season. The female lays 1000–4000 eggs in a large clump of frogspawn. After the eggs have been deposited in the water they are fertilized by the male, so that they can produce tadpoles.

It is a good thing that female frogs lay so many eggs: most of them never develop into adult frogs. The enemies of the frog are many, and include snakes, mammals such as foxes, otters, hedgehogs and rats, fish such as the pike and perch, and birds such as herons, hawks, seagulls, ducks and geese. Added to this, frogs are attacked by many diseases and parasites (creatures that live on or inside other animals). The frog's greatest enemy, though, is man, who especially over the last 20 years has drained and filled in many ponds and ditches, places where frogs used to live but now cannot. The water in many ponds has been polluted, and the use of insecticides (chemical sprays and the like designed to kill insects) cuts down frogs' food-supply and can cause other damage.

If you want to help the frog, keep your garden pond clean and make sure it is not choked with weeds. Have lots of plants growing round the edge to

Frogs are amphibians not reptiles

provide shade and shelter. Use insecticides as little as possible, and, if you do collect frogspawn in the spring to watch it hatch into tadpoles and see how the tadpoles change into frogs, please make sure that, as soon as the little creatures have grown their hind legs, you release them into the pond or lake where you found the frogspawn.

The Snail

All that most people know about snails is that they move very slowly and that they can be pests in the garden. There is much more than that to them, however. Some are still well under 1 mm long when fully grown, but they are relatives of the octopus, the pearl oyster and the monster giant squid, which grows to a size of 20 m across and battles with sperm whales 5000 m down in the ocean depths. Snails in times gone by were often cruelly treated, particularly in the preparation of folk medicines and charms. Some country people used to think that if they swallowed snails it would stop them coughing!

Snails are members of the group of animals called molluscs, which includes 60,000 species. Molluscs are such

The humble snail is related to the octopus

Snails are molluscs, soft-bodied animals that make mobile homes of shell

Shell made of chalk with a little protein

successful creatures that they are found nearly everywhere, on land and in water. They have many different designs. Most belong to a sub-group called *Gastropoda*, and, although many have shells protecting their soft bodies, others, such as slugs, do not.

A snail's body consists of a head that can be moved very easily and is packed with sense organs. Behind the head are the internal organs (heart, liver, intestines, and so on) surrounded by a covering of soft tissue. The upper part of this covering is called the 'mantle' and hangs down round the body to enclose a hollow with a damp lining that acts as the lungs and absorbs oxygen for breathing. The lower part of the soft covering is enlarged into a muscular foot which contains a mouth fitted with rows of horny teeth (the

'radula'). This curious design, which allows the snail to gnaw its food with its foot, explains the Latin name *Gastropoda*, which means 'stomach feet'. A snail's blood is not red but colourless and circulates through blood-vessels pumped by a heart with 3 chambers.

The shell is made up of chemicals secreted by the mantle. It is made up of a small amount of a kind of protein mixed with a large amount of chalk. Because the snail needs a source of chalky chemicals, you will not find many snails on acid soils.

The biggest land-snail is the *giant African snail* (which makes a most interesting and cheap pet for a keen young biologist). Its body may be over 20 cm long, and it can weigh as much as 250 gm. The Japanese army brought this snail to the Pacific area during the Second World War as a source of fresh food. At the end of the war the American troops accidentally imported the species into the United States.

43

A pest: the giant African snail

Because the giant African breeds very quickly and is very destructive, it soon became a problem in farming areas. It has been estimated that one snail can produce around 11 million offspring over a period of 5 years. Attempts have been made to control the vegetarian giant African snail by introducing species of carnivorous snails which prey upon it.

There are 80 species of land-snail in Britain, of which the biggest is the *Roman* or *edible snail*, which occurs in limestone areas in the south and is rather rare. Its body is up to 10 cm long and it weighs up to 90 gm. This snail was introduced by the Romans as food, and has a strong, round, creamy-coloured shell. The *common garden snail* has a round shell that is pale brown with up to 5 dark bands and measures about 35 mm across. Like most snails, it is active mainly at night. During the day it retreats to its favourite damp spot and has a nap. In the winter or if the weather is unusually hot and dry, snails seal up the opening of their shell with a thick sticky film to save the moisture inside.

Snails are 'hermaphrodites', which means that they are not male or female but *both*, so they can *all* lay eggs. However, they still have to mate. During mating, which usually occurs at night in summer, they come together and stab one another with a tiny barbed arrow made of chalk. This injects spermatozoa, living male organisms which then set about fertilizing the female eggs contained within each snail. The eggs, which are tiny and white, are laid in batches of up to 40 in holes in the soil. After 4 weeks or so, perfect mini-snails emerge.

Other land-snails which you may come across in the garden include the *moss snail*, which has a light brown body and a long cone-shaped shell around 6 mm long that is shiny and pale to dark-brown in colour. This snail loves damp moss, piles of dead leaves and compost-heaps. The *tree snail* has a long, cone-shaped, brownish or greenish shell about 10 mm long, and may be seen on treetrunks or dry stone walls in gardens. The *white-lipped banded snail* has a shiny, thin, round shell about 17 mm wide and 20 mm high, slightly flattened on the sides. The shell-colour varies, but is often yellow, with up to 5 dark bands. The snail's body is greenish-grey. The *dark-lipped banded snail* has a much thicker and more rounded shell about 22 mm wide and 25 mm high; the colour varies from yellow to brown and the number of bands varies too. The body is greyish-yellow. The colours and markings of banded snails' shells depend on where the snails live, helping them blend into their surroundings more easily. They are darker in woodland than in gardens because woodland colours are darker than garden colours. My favourite garden snail is the tiny (5 mm high and wide) *garlic glass snail*, which emits a strong smell of garlic if upset or handled.

One of the snail's great enemies, the thrush

Snails can live for up to 10 years, but they have lots of enemies. The most famous is the thrush, which uses a stone to crack open their shells and eat their soft bodies.

A snail 'family snapshot'